Communities

Living Near a River

By Joanne Winne

Welcome Books

Children's Press

A Div
New York   dney

Photo Credits: Cover © L. Kolvoord/The Image Works; pp. 5, 7, 9,11, 13, 15 © National Geographic; p. 17 © L. Kolvoord/The Image Works; p.19 © Index Stock Imagery; p. 21© Dammrich/The Image Works
Contributing Editor: Jennifer Ceaser
Book Design: Nelson Sa

Visit Children's Press on the Internet at:
http://publishing.grolier.com

Cataloging-in-Publication Data

Winne, Joanne
  Living near a river / by Joanne Winne.
    p. cm. — (Communities)
  Includes bibliographical references and index.
  Summary: This book discusses the lives of children who
live near various rivers in the world.
  ISBN 0-516-23302-5 (lib. bdg.) — ISBN 0-516-23502-8 (pbk.)
  1. Rivers—Juvenile literature 2. Stream ecology—
Juvenile literature [1. River life 2. Rivers] I. Title
II. Series
  GF63.W56 2000
  307—dc21

00-024037

Contents

My name is Abu (ah-**bu**).

I live near the Nile River in Egypt (ee-**jipt**).

4

5

I live in a **village** along the river.

Many **palm trees** grow around my house.

7

My family has a **sailboat**.

I like to sail along the river.

The river is very quiet at **dusk**.

9

My name is Marco.

This is my pet parrot.

I live near the Amazon (**am**-ah-zon) River in Brazil.

11

I live in a fishing village.

My father catches fish to sell at the market.

He ties up his boat to a **dock**.

13

I like to sit on my father's boat.

We take a ride down the river.

15

My name is Josh.

I live near the Colorado River in Texas.

17

This is my **neighborhood**.

My house looks out over the river.

19

These are two of my friends.

They are trying to catch **minnows**.

There are many things to discover in the river.

New Words

dock (**dok**) place where people keep
   their boats
dusk (**dusk**) the time just before it gets
   dark
minnows (**min**-ohz) very small fish that
   live in rivers and lakes
neighborhood (**nay**-ber-hud) the streets
   and houses around where you live
palm trees (**pahlm treez**) tall trees with
   no branches and many large leaves
sailboat (**sayl**-boht) a boat with a piece
   of cloth called a sail; it moves by the
   power of the wind
village (**vil**-ij) a group of houses, a small
   town

22

To Find Out More

Books
Living Near a River
by Allan Fowler
Children's Press

The River
by Gallimard Jeunesse
Scholastic

Web Sites
Exploring the Vast Amazon
http://tqjunior.thinkquest.org
Discover the people, animals, and plants that live along the Amazon. Then take the Amazon quiz!

Wild Egypt
http://touregypt.net/wildegypt/nile1.htm
Check out all the amazing sights along the Nile River. Find out more about the cities, people, and animals that use the river.

Index

About the Author
Joanne Winne taught fourth grade for nine years and currently writes and edits books for children. She lives in Hoboken, New Jersey.

Reading Consultants
Kris Flynn, Coordinator, Small School District Literacy, The San Diego County Office of Education

Shelly Forys, Certified Reading Recovery Specialist, W.J. Zahnow Elementary School, Waterloo, IL

Peggy McNamara, Professor, Bank Street College of Education, Reading and Literacy Program